These picture books of Mediæval and Renaissance to Early XIX Century Sculptors are designed to encourage a wider general appreciation of sculpture in England rather than to stimulate any scholarly discussions of attribution or detailed researches on origin and influences. With this end in view we hope that the whole treatment will be found simple and straightforward.

Despite the enormous destruction wrought by time, war and iconoclasm in England, there is still a great deal of very beautiful Mediæval work to be found in the country if we set out to look for it. This series of details offers an insight into the sensitivity and high quality to be found in English sculpture during the period. The fact of this quality may come as a surprise to many observers, and although subjects have naturally been chosen from among the best examples still extant, there is no reason to doubt that when they were carved a reasonably high percentage of a similar standard was to be found.

UNIFORM WITH THIS VOLUME

Sculpture in England: Renaissance to Early XIX Century

SCULPTURE IN ENGLAND:

Mediæval

BY

H. D. MOLESWORTH

PUBLISHED FOR

THE BRITISH COUNCIL

BY LONGMANS, GREEN AND CO

LONDON   NEW YORK   TORONTO

LONGMANS, GREEN AND CO. LTD.
6 & 7 Clifford Street, London, W.1.
Also at Melbourne and Cape Town

LONGMANS, GREEN AND CO. INC.
55 Fifth Avenue, New York, 3

LONGMANS, GREEN AND CO.
215 Victoria Street, Toronto, 1

ORIENT LONGMANS LTD.
Bombay   Calcutta   Madras

First published 1951

BRITISH COUNCIL'S CODE NAME: SCULPTURE ONE

PRINTED IN GREAT BRITAIN BY JARROLD AND SONS LTD., NORWICH

ACKNOWLEDGMENTS

It is far from easy to get good photographs of sculpture. We are therefore particularly grateful to those institutions and scholars who have helped us so generously. Individual acknowledgments will be found at the end of the notes, but since the whole production is really a combined operation we should at the outset record our appreciation of the unstinting collaboration received among others from the Directors and Staffs of the Victoria and Albert Museum, the British Museum, the Warburg Institute, the Courtauld Institute, and the National Buildings Record. The contribution of the Warburg Institute with its magnificent collection of photographs, mostly by Mr. O. Fein, has been especially generous; we also acknowledge with pleasure the co-operation of Dr. G. Zarnecki of the Courtauld Institute of Art, who prepared the notes.

WHEN LOOKING AT THE MEDIÆVAL sculpture of any Christian country we have to remember that its basic spirit and inspiration were international, like the Church which it served. Such local developments of style as we see in a survey of this kind are, therefore, variations on a general theme rather than elements with a direct evolution of their own.

We have an admirable example in the Easby Cross, *plates* IV and V, with its stylized beasts in vine scrolls. Such a conception originated perhaps in the Near East, but Northern Europeans seized upon the idea and moulded it to an art of their own. The English certainly delighted in this convention, and as we can see in the details from the ivory Tau Cross, *plate* XI, or those from the Gloucester Candlestick, *plate* X, the eleventh and twelfth centuries were still enthralled by it, although the treatment had become more elaborate. There has been much speculation as to why such a form of decoration was popular; efforts have been made to assess its meaning to the contemporary mind, but perhaps we need no further explanation than a delight in intricacy of pattern, coupled with the manifest pleasure in natural things shown by a community living at a slow tempo and in intimate contact with nature.

This Romanesque style was not, of course, limited to England; in default of direct evidence, it is often difficult to be absolutely sure where certain objects came from, especially in the case of later pieces. Examples generally held to be English are perhaps characterized by a more vigorous alertness in the figures coupled with rather less stylized and decorative handling of the ornament. But with the evolution of Gothic—an evolution, of course, coinciding with the establishment of a developed 'English' social and political organization—a more clearly defined English contribution can be noted. In the figures on the small ivory box, *plate* XIX, in the Salting and Grandisson ivories, or in the Westminster and Lincoln figures, there is a quiet, restrained, gentle, almost lyrical quality. The atmosphere of 'good breeding' without elaboration or flourish is already in the tradition of English reticence. We have only to look to Chaucer for contemporary evidence that the quality was consciously appreciated in the fourteenth century.

The remarkable 'ideal' quality of the sculptures of the thirteenth century, which coincided with the highest development of the chivalrous traditions of

7

feudalism, showed some decline in spiritual approach, if not in technical quality, during the fourteenth century, and became even less satisfactory by the fifteenth. This movement was common to the whole of Europe, with the exception of Italy, where the Renaissance was under way. In England the decadence was unhappily rather more marked than elsewhere; the decline has been assigned to a variety of causes, emphasis being distributed between the Black Death, the civil and foreign wars, and the whole course of social development. It was finally and forcibly emphasized in England by the iconoclasm of the Reformation in the early sixteenth century.

Even before the Reformation, however, there is evidence that leading patrons in England called upon foreign craftsmen. This influence is illustrated here by the effigy of Henry VII, *plate* LV, which may be the work of the Italian Pietro Torrigiano.

Passing from the particular of English sculpture to the question of general appreciation, the great disadvantage for a piece of sculpture as a work of art is that it is almost always something else as well, and frequently that functional purpose may be more readily understood or more assertive than the æsthetic significance of the carving. This disadvantage can certainly arise, for example, where the sculpture forms part of some larger architectural whole, as over doors or windows or on the tympana or façades of churches and cathedrals. In such cases most people see the building as one entity and miss the special detailed merits of the sculpture unless their minds are directly concentrated upon it.

But it is not only in relation to some wider physical whole—whether building or landscape—that sculptures may get 'lost'. There is frequently an emotional, spiritual, or intellectual association in the object, which may be very distracting. In day-to-day life sculpture is probably most commonly met with in the form of monuments or tombs or in religious icons of one sort or another. In such cases it is only natural that the 'purpose' of the sculpture may have strong claims of its own, which may have more or less effect according to the individual. A deeply religious Christian may well not look at a representation of the Virgin or a saint with the dispassionate æsthetic appraisal of someone of another faith. In the case of monuments, we are almost invariably brought up to think of the historical or personal associations: it is So-and-so's tomb, or this records such-and-such a battle. It is rarely that the merits of the sculpture immediately come to mind.

In making these points we are in no way attempting to deny the use and value of sculpture for these various ends, but by stating the fact of this frequently dual personality we hope to clear the way for a more deliberate appreciation of both the historical and the æsthetic qualities of a subject. We are, however, by no means confined to monuments or buildings for examples of fine sculpture; and these illustrations, which have been drawn from a wide variety of sources, certainly show that great beauty in sculpture is to be found in many, often unexpected, places. Consecutive details shown in the plates may vary from part of an ivory, perhaps only an inch high, contrasted with over-life-size figures from a cathedral front. Juxtaposition of this kind also establishes that sculpture need not be dependent on size for its artistic qualities. Consideration of details proves that we need to look and look again if we are going to appreciate to the full what is available to us.

This question of 'looking' at sculpture, as at any other art form, is naturally of first importance to appreciation, but with sculpture the difficulties are emphasized; understanding is seldom automatic, or readily come by without some effort on our part.

All appreciation is to some degree a matter of habit or conditioning, but of sculpture few communities encounter fine examples every day, or even good reproductions in sympathetic material. Again, sculpture does not offer the readily assimilated presentation generally offered by a work in two dimensions. A painting can present at a single glance what the artist has in mind. A piece of sculpture may be visible from a variety of angles, and in different lights, each of which may affect its interpretation. Looking at sculpture is therefore likely to be a more exacting process. Memory has a large part to play, for while the eye may be fixed upon or moving over any one surface from a particular angle, the impression conveyed to the mind is likely to depend partly upon appreciation of what has already been seen from other angles.

In this difficulty the good photograph can often offer invaluable help. It can be virtually the interpretation of an interpretation. Not only does it translate the three dimensions into two, but it also presents a static, insistent, assimilated view of the object. This is, of course, necessarily subjective; but it can at least be free from any distracting factors, such as changing light, bad light, or the functional purposes already referred to.

It would naturally be easy to choose many sets of fifty photographs illustrating the passing centuries of British mediæval art, so that any selection is bound to be arbitrary. In view of this fact we have allowed ourselves to take advantage of particularly good photographs for the very reason that they are good photographs, affording, as we felt, a just interpretation of the piece and period concerned. The choice has also been influenced by the availability of the originals to a normal visiting public. A very great number of the examples chosen are to be found in London. We hope this will make it possible for readers attracted by some particular reproduction to look at the original whenever they may happen to come to England or to be in the metropolis.

PLATE I: Roof boss, XIII century

PLATE III: Detail, Franks Casket, VII–VIII century

PLATE II: Head, ? I century

PLATE IV:
Easby Cross,
VIII–IX century

PLATE V:
Easby Cross,
VIII–IX century

PLATE VII: Grave-stone, XI century

PLATE VI: Saint, VIII century

PLATE VIII: Christ in Majesty, XI century

PLATE IX: Virgin and Child, XI century

PLATE XI: St. Michael, XII century

PLATE X: Figure with beasts, XII century

PLATES XIV, XV: Details, pastoral staff, XII century

PLATES XVI, XVII: Details, Chichester reliefs, XII century

PLATE XVIII: Centaurs, XII century

PLATE XIX: Monks, XII century

PLATE XX: Capital, XII century

PLATE XXI: Tympanum, XII century

PLATE XXII: Capital, XII century

PLATE XXIII: Relief, XII century

PLATE XXIV: St. Peter, XII century

PLATE XXV: Moses, XIII century

PLATES XXVI, XXVIIa, XXVIIb: Saints, XIII century

PLATES XXVIII, XXIX:
Annunciation,
XIII century

PLATES XXX, XXXI: Angels, XIII century

PLATE XXXIII: Henry III, XIII century

PLATE XXXII: Bishop, XIII century

PLATE XXXIV: Knight, XIII century

PLATE XXXV: Knight, XIV century

PLATE XXXVII: Detail, Grandisson Diptych, XIV century

PLATE XXXVI: Salting Diptych, XIV century

PLATE XXXVIII: Corbels, XIV century

PLATE XXXIX: Seated figures, XIV century

PLATE XL: Detail, Adoration, XIV century

PLATE XLI: Richard II, XIV century

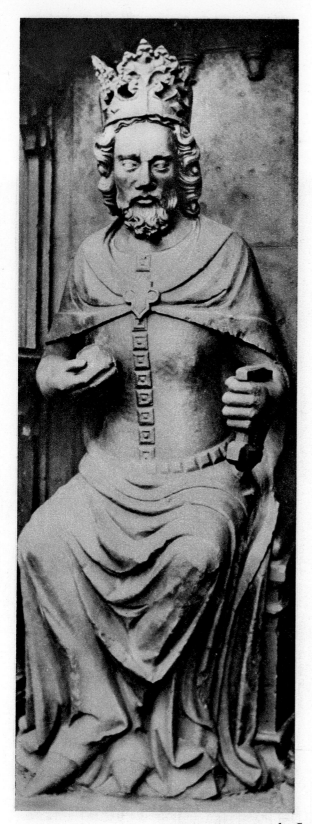 

PLATES XLIIIa, XLIIIb: Seated kings, XIV century

PLATE XLII: Annunciation, XIV century

PLATE XLIV: Annunciation, XIV century

PLATE XLV: Resurrection, XIV century

PLATE XLVI:
St. Christopher,
XV century

PLATE XLVII:
Virgin and Child,
XV century

PLATE XLVIII: Effigy, XV century

PLATE XLIX: Effigy, XV century

PLATE L:
Mourner,
XV century

PLATE LI:
St. John,
XVI century

PLATE LII:
Philosopher,
XVI century

PLATE LIII:
St. Agatha,
XVI century

PLATE LIV: Bust, XVI century

PLATE LV: Henry VII, XVI century

PLATE LVI: Roof boss, XVI century

Notes on the Plates

FRONT COVER
Roof boss (stone: first half of the XIV century) *East walk of cloister, Norwich Cathedral.*

Soon after the introduction of ribbed vaulting in the XII century the stone of the rib-junction, or keystone, began to be enriched with sculpture. These keystones, usually called bosses, received their most sumptuous decoration in the later Gothic period. One of the most important series of bosses, numbering nearly 400, is at Norwich Cathedral, where the original Norman cloister was replaced by a new one during the XIV and XV centuries. The example here illustrated, carved with a foliate head, is one of the simplest in the Norwich series, yet it is full of beauty. The circular composition of the carving underlines and crowns the junction of the numerous ribs.

PLATE I
Roof boss (stone: *c.* 1250) *Angel Choir aisle, Lincoln Cathedral.*

In this admirable and vigorous composition three monsters are biting each other. Their long tails wind round the ribs of the vaulting, joining them like the knots of a rope. The sculptor has achieved an extraordinary impression of violent movement, but subordinated it to the architectural function of the keystone, i.e. the joining of the different ribs in one whole.

PLATE II
Head (stone, height 8 in.: ? I century) *Gloucester Museum.*

There is very little evidence of the existence of monumental sculpture in Britain before the Roman conquest. The Gloucester head shows Roman influence, particularly in the realistic treatment of the hair, but is predominantly a Celtic work. This is evident in the geometrical stylization, strikingly illustrated by the modelling of the bulging eyes and triangular nose.

PLATE III
Assault on the house of Egil the Archer; detail of the cover of the Franks Casket (whalebone: length of the whole casket 9 in.: VII–VIII century) *British Museum.*

During the religious renaissance in the VII and VIII centuries there was an astonishing blossoming of the arts in both the south and north of Anglo-Saxon England. The Franks Casket (named after Sir Augustus Franks, Keeper of the British Museum, who acquired it for the Museum in 1867) is one of the most celebrated examples of the sculpture of the period.
The casket displays a mixture of pagan and Christian subjects such as Romulus and Remus and the Adoration of the Magi. The various episodes from northern sagas, such as the one on the cover, are particularly difficult to name, in spite of the runic inscriptions.
The style of the carving, which gives the human figures a form so geometrical as to be almost abstract, is characteristic of northern tendencies in Northumbrian art.

PLATES IV and V
Fragments of a stone cross-shaft from Easby, Yorkshire (VIII or early IX century) *Victoria and Albert Museum.*

Nothing could show better the classical heritage of Northumbrian art than the figure sculpture on four surviving fragments of the Easby Cross. The main subject is Christ and the Apostles. The side carved with representations of birds and animals perched among branches and foliage shows a curious transformation of Mediterranean models into something more stylized. It has been suggested that Carolingian ivories brought from the Continent could have been used as models by the Northumbrian sculptors.

PLATE VI
Stone figure of a saint (height *c.* 3 ft.: late VIII century) *Castor Church, Northamptonshire.*

This sculpture, which probably formed part of the reredos of an altar, is a brave attempt by an Anglo-Saxon sculptor to show the roundness of the body and the forward movement of the figure, combined with a dignity of pose and a gravity of expression.

PLATE VII
Viking grave-stone (width 3 ft.: early XI century) *Guildhall Museum, London.*

This stone, found on the site of St. Paul's Church-yard, is one of the finest examples of pagan Viking art. The roundness of Anglo-Saxon sculpture is replaced here by a flat design, and the animal fighting with a serpent is transformed into an intricate geometrical pattern, with spirals incised on its body.

PLATES VIII and IX
Christ in Majesty and the Virgin and Child enthroned (oval reliefs in morse ivory: height 4 in.: early XI century) *Victoria and Albert Museum.*

These are examples of the vigorous art of the 'Winchester School' which flourished in southern England during the late X and XI centuries and is seen at its best in the pen drawings of illuminated manuscripts. The influence of pen-drawing on the carving of ivory is here seen in the linear treatment of the rich stylized draperies.

PLATE X
Detail of Gloucester Candlestick (gilt bell-metal: total height 23 in.: *c.* 1110) *Victoria and Albert Museum.*

The inscription on the candlestick shows that it was given to the Abbey (now the Cathedral) of St. Peter at Gloucester by Peter, Abbot of Gloucester from 1104 to 1113. The symbols of the Evangelists and small figures of men, animals, and monsters climbing in the foliage or fighting each other give an impression of dynamic move-ment and richness.

PLATE XI
St. Michael fighting the Dragon. Detail of the head of a tau cross (walrus ivory: height $2\frac{1}{4}$ in.: first half of XII century) *Victoria and Albert Museum.*

The staffs used by bishops and abbots in the Middle Ages were often shaped at the head like the Greek letter *tau* and were thus called tau crosses. These heads were usually of ivory. This example is of particular beauty. The triumphant figure of St. Michael with his wings widely spread is shown in violent forward movement towards the dragon's head. The monster's body forms the circular

frame of the composition and is covered with decorative motives of beads and leaves.

PLATES XII and XIII
Adoration of the Magi (whalebone carved in relief: height $14\frac{1}{4}$ in.: XII century) *Victoria and Albert Museum.*

This beautiful ivory has been claimed for France, Ireland, and Belgium, but so far no conclusive evidence of its origin or date has been produced. Certain similarities to early XII-century English illuminated manuscripts suggest that it is perhaps of English workmanship.

PLATES XIV and XV
The dead Christ and the Nativity. Details of the head of a pastoral staff (ivory: height $4\frac{1}{2}$ in.: XII century) *Victoria and Albert Museum.*

This powerful carving illustrates scenes from the Nativity and Passion, and the contrast between the episodes enhances the dramatic effect. The sculp-tor's technical skill reveals a command of expression which ranges from lyrical serenity to the agony of death.

PLATES XVI and XVII
Heads of Christ, Martha, Mary, and an Apostle, from the stone panel showing the Raising of Lazarus (the whole panel 3 ft. 6 in. square: XII century) *Chichester Cathedral.*

There has been a great deal of controversy about the date of this carving, and of the second Chiches-ter panel, which shows Christ and the Apostles coming to Mary's house. They have been attri-buted to the XI or XII century, the latter now being the generally accepted date. The grave emotional content of the carvings is exceptional even for this period.

PLATE XVIII
Two centaurs, from a design on an oval box of walrus ivory (height of box 3 in., length $2\frac{1}{2}$ in.: XII century) *Victoria and Albert Museum.*

Creatures of Greek and Roman mythology such as sirens, gryphons, and centaurs were very popular as subjects of mediæval art, their composite nature apparently appealing strongly to the imagination of the age. Here centaurs with drawn bows are used in a decorative and strictly symmetrical manner.

PLATE XIX
Two figures of monks from a design on an oval box of walrus ivory (height 2⅝ in.: XII century) *Victoria and Albert Museum.*

Many mediæval legends have been forgotten, and it is often impossible to identify a scene such as this one. The figures display an intimate charm and sincerity of feeling characteristic of the best Romanesque art. The style, more pacific than in some of the preceding examples, perhaps heralds the Gothic.

PLATE XX
Animals playing musical instruments (stone: *c.* 1120) *Capital in the crypt of Canterbury Cathedral.*

The renaissance in stone sculpture on the Continent in the first quarter of the XII century extended to England, where a great southern school flourished, probably originating at Canterbury. The subjects used to decorate the capitals in the crypt are often full of violence; others are humorous illustrations of fables.

PLATE XXI
Apostles (stone: nearly life size: *c.* 1160) *Tympanum of south porch of Malmesbury Abbey, Wiltshire.*

This sculpture is truly monumental in style; the figures have become plastic and three-dimensional, as if freed from the bonds of stone. There are six apostles on each side of the porch; over the entrance Christ is shown in glory supported by angels. The five orders of the doorway are carved with scenes from the Old and New Testaments.

PLATE XXII
Fighting animals (stone: *c.* 1120) *Capital in the crypt of Canterbury Cathedral.*

Scenes depicting violent fights between monsters were common in the Romanesque art of Western Europe; in England, perhaps as a result of Viking influence, they take a particularly dynamic form.

PLATE XXIII
Noah building his Ark (stone: height 3 ft.: *c.* 1150) *West front, Lincoln Cathedral.*

One of a series of rectangular panels in relief added when the west front was rebuilt after the fire of 1141. Though some were disturbed by later alterations, many are still in their original positions. Carved with subjects from the Old Testament and the Last Judgment, they show a less detailed and more monumental treatment.

PLATE XXIV
Seal of Cathedral Priory (XII century) *Winchester.*

The seated figure of St. Peter with his keys is shown on the plate many times enlarged; in spite of this, the figure does not lose its peculiar beauty. The figure is light and elegant and highly decorative. This photograph suggests the study of seals not only for their historical interest but also for their artistic beauty.

PLATE XXV
Moses. Detail of a life-size statue (stone: *c.* 1200) *Museum of the Philosophical Society, York.*

This statue, together with nine others, came from St. Mary's Abbey, York. It is a column-statue of the type popularized by the early Gothic porches of the cathedrals of the Ile-de-France, notably Saint-Denis and Chartres.

PLATES XXVI, XXVIIa and XXVIIb
Statues of Saints (stone: life size: *c.* 1240) *West front, Wells Cathedral.*

It was said of XIII-century cathedrals that they are scholastic encyclopædias carved in stone; the saying is true of Wells Cathedral. There were originally 180 statues and many reliefs covering the whole of the west front. The general plan covers the story from the Creation to the Last Judgment, with the Virgin Mary as the central composition above the main entrance, and with Christ in Majesty high up on the gable. The statues, four of which are illustrated here, are carved in the round and placed in canopied niches. Some of them represent the ancestors of Christ and others are figures of saints.

PLATES XXVIII and XXIX
The Annunciation (stone: life size: *c.* 1250)
Chapter House, Westminster Abbey.

The figures are placed on either side of the entrance. They are later than those on the west front of Wells Cathedral, from which they derive. Both these Westminster figures are freed from their architectural background. Their hands are carved in graceful gestures, and their bodies turn or lean back. The Archangel Gabriel blesses the Virgin.

PLATE XXX
Figure of censing angel (stone: nearly life size: *c.* 1255) *East side of south transept, Westminster Abbey.*

This angel is one of two in the south transept; there is a similar pair in the north transept. Their shape is artificial, as they fill triangular spandrels in the triforium, but the effect is exquisite. The figures come to life and have a swinging movement; they are often rightly compared with classical sculpture.

PLATE XXXI
Angel with pipe and tabor (stone: nearly life size: *c.* 1280) *Angel Choir, Lincoln Cathedral.*

These reliefs of angels decorate the spandrels of the triforium arches and give the choir its name. One group, connected with the Last Judgment, is shown weighing souls; one angel holds a sword and another presents a soul to Christ. The other group is of angels in heaven carrying crowns, books, and scrolls; some, among them the one here illustrated, play musical instruments. The figures in the first group are stern; those in the second express happiness and joy.

PLATE XXXII
Detail of effigy on tomb of Bishop and Chancellor William de Kilkenny (Purbeck marble: life size: *c.* 1256) *Ely Cathedral.*

This 'idealized' figure represents the bishop in his robes, giving a benediction; the figure is flanked by censing angels. No attempt at portraiture is yet made.

PLATE XXXIII
Detail, effigy on tomb of Henry III (bronze gilt: life size: 1291–2) *Westminster Abbey.*

This effigy, and that of Eleanor of Castile, first queen of Edward I, were executed at King Edward's order by William Torel, a London goldsmith. King Henry's effigy was the first life-size bronze figure in English art, and set a fashion for royal monuments in this metal.

PLATE XXXIV
Seal of Robert Fitzwalter (early XIII century) *British Museum.*

Seals with galloping riders became common from the reign of Henry II onwards, the Great Royal Seal of that king being of that type. These representations on seals were later successfully imitated in stone, as comparison with the following plate shows.

PLATE XXXV
Detail of the tomb of Aymer de Valence, Earl of Pembroke (stone painted in imitation of marble: soon after 1324) *Westminster Abbey.*

Aymer de Valence's tomb belongs to the group of canopied monuments which became the fashion at the end of the XIII century with the erection of the tomb of Edmund Crouchback, Earl of Lancaster and brother of Edward I, also in Westminster Abbey. While the Earl of Pembroke himself is represented lying with his hands folded in prayer, the relief on the canopy represents a knight galloping on horseback in remembrance of the earl's warlike life. This relief is an admirable expression of the spirit of the age of chivalry.

PLATE XXXVI
The Virgin and Child and Christ giving a blessing (ivory diptych: height 8½ in.: *c.* 1300) *Victoria and Albert Museum.*

This celebrated diptych in the Salting Collection of the Museum has a monumental quality suggestive of stone sculpture. There are no unnecessary details, and attention is concentrated on the faces; the folds of the draperies are logical in arrangement and harmonious in effect.

PLATE XXXVII

The Annunciation. Detail of ivory diptych (total height 9½ in.: middle of XIV century) *British Museum.*

Only half of this diptych, showing the Annunciation with the figure of St. John the Baptist below, is in the British Museum; the other half, showing the Coronation of the Virgin and the figure of St. John the Evangelist, is in the Louvre. The diptych may have been made for John Grandisson, Bishop of Exeter (1327–69). The Annunciation, although not remarkable for inspiration, is typical of the more popular art of the ivory carvers; it is delicately worked and has great elegance of movement.

PLATE XXXVIII

Corbels on Percy tomb (stone: middle of XIV century) *Beverley Minster.*

The growing interest of Gothic artists in realism was shown not only in greater understanding of the human form and of movement, but also in facial expression, as seen here in the heads of a bishop and a king supporting a figure of King David.

PLATE XXXIX

Warrior and King (stone: above life size: *c.* 1345) *West front of Exeter Cathedral.*

The dramatic quality of the sculpture of the Decorated Style was achieved at Exeter by contorted gestures, crossed legs, and faces expressing violent emotion.

PLATE XL

Adoration of the Magi. Detail of the reredos (stone: nearly life size: *c.* 1350) *Christchurch Priory, Hampshire.*

The reredos at the back of the high altar at Christchurch is very close in style to the Exeter figures (previous plate). It has certainly the same quality of exaltation expressed by contorted poses and gestures. Yet it also has a certain lyrical feeling, shown by the eagerness of the kneeling Magus as he presents his gift to the Child, who is happily playing on his Mother's knee.

PLATE XLI

Detail, tomb effigy of Richard II (bronze gilt: life size: 1395–7) *Westminster Abbey.*

In 1395 two London coppersmiths, Nicholas Broker and Godfrey Prest, were commissioned to make effigies of Richard II and his first queen, Anne of Bohemia. These effigies are of outstanding interest; they are courageous, sincere, and unflattering attempts at portraiture. The king's features correspond very closely to those in his painted portrait in the choir of Westminster Abbey.

PLATE XLII

The Annunciation (painted oak: height 4 ft.: XIV century) *Corporation of Vicars Choral, Wells.*

The tall, youthful figure of the Virgin has a lyrical charm; she takes a step backwards as the Archangel Gabriel approaches. Gabriel is an elegant, worldly figure rather than a heavenly messenger. The stress on elegance and the neglect of individual expression become obvious weaknesses in later Gothic sculpture.

PLATES XLIIIa and XLIIIb

Statues of Kings (stone: above life size: *c.* 1380) *West front of Lincoln Cathedral.*

Here the gestures made by the figures are still varied but no longer dramatic. Greater stress is laid on physical beauty, on the arrangement of the hair, and on details of costume.

PLATES XLIV

The Annunciation (alabaster: 15⅞ in. by 10⅞ in.: XIV century) *Victoria and Albert Museum.*

The exploitation of quarries in the Midlands made possible the development and commercial production of alabaster carvings in the XIV and XV centuries. Nottingham was the chief centre of the industry, which acquired a European reputation. This Annunciation is one of the gentler and simpler works carved before the establishment of mass production.

PLATE XLV

The Resurrection (alabaster: height 18 in.: XIV century) *Victoria and Albert Museum.*

Another carving of the same type and quality as those of the Annunciation shown in Plate XLII.

PLATE XLVI
St. Christopher (alabaster: height 3 ft. 3 in.: XV century) *Victoria and Albert Museum.*

This saint is one of the largest figures in alabaster; the sculpture is a dignified and touching treatment of the episode of his carrying the Child across the river, and has more individual quality than the average mass-produced work in this material.

PLATE XLVII
Virgin and Child (alabaster: height 2 ft. 8 in.: c. 1400) *Nottingham Museum.*

This sculpture comes from Flawford in Nottinghamshire, where it was buried at the time of the Reformation to save it from destruction. The statue is a typical example of competent alabaster production. Similar figures could at one time probably have been found in almost every church.

PLATE XLVIII
Tomb effigy of Richard Beauchamp, Earl of Warwick (bronze gilt: life size: c. 1453) *St. Mary's Church, Warwick.*

This is a magnificent monument based on Burgundian models; the bronze effigy lies on a high base which is surrounded by the smaller figures of mourners (see Plate L). The effigy, executed by William Austen in London, is a remarkable work of art. The wrinkled forehead and veined hands reflect an increasing interest in portraiture.

PLATE XLIX
Tomb effigy of Alice, Duchess of Suffolk (alabaster: life size: c. 1480) *Ewelme Church, Oxfordshire.*

The realism of Gothic tomb-portraiture reached its height in the XV century. The severe, determined, almost ascetic face of the Duchess of Suffolk shows that sculptors and their patrons attached importance to a close likeness.

PLATE L
A mourner. Bronze figure from the tomb of Richard Beauchamp (see Plate XLVIII).

Figures, probably of the Earl's relatives, stand in niches round the base of the monument, as if attending the funeral. Real grief is expressed by this figure with its head bent and a loose robe covering even the hands.

PLATE LI
St. John the Evangelist (bronze: c. 1510) *Grille of Tomb of King Henry VII, Westminster Abbey.*

Only six of the statuettes which once decorated the grille enclosing the tomb still survive. In this example the dress is richly folded, providing strong contrasts of light and shade. Such preoccupation with picturesque effect was a characteristic of late Gothic sculpture. It has been suggested that the figures on this grille were adapted from an earlier chapel designed for Henry VI but never completed.

PLATES LII and LIII
A Philosopher and St. Agatha (stone: half life size: early XVI century) *Henry VII's Chapel, Westminster Abbey.*

The chapel was founded in 1502–3 and completed in 1519 and is a superb example of late Gothic architecture. The rich architectural sculpture of this chapel, illustrated here by two examples, shows contrasting effects of light and shade, complicated draperies and picturesque costumes; its technical skill is extraordinary, but this late Gothic sculpture was already fighting a losing battle with the rapidly spreading art of the Italian Renaissance.

PLATE LIV
Sir Gilbert Talbot of Grafton Manor, Worcestershire (bust in terracotta: English, under Italian influence: early XVI century). *Victoria and Albert Museum.*

This bust, traditionally held to be a portrait of the Talbot who fought at the Battle of Bosworth (1485), makes a most interesting comparison with the following bust of King Henry VII. It shows not only local development based on Italian work, but also a prevailing interest in lifelike portraiture as opposed to the more symbolic or stylized production of preceding centuries.

PLATE LV

Henry VII (bust in painted and gilded terracotta: Italian, by a Florentine sculptor, perhaps Pietro Torrigiano, 1472–1528). First quarter of the XVI century. *Victoria and Albert Museum.*

This is one of a group of three busts perhaps made for the royal palace. Torrigiano was brought over to England to execute the bronze bust of Henry VII in Westminster Abbey; the style of the terracotta is so close to his work that the attribution is almost certainly correct. In any event the bust shows the establishment, by the XVI century, of the Italian domination of Northern European art.

PLATE LVI

Roof boss (wood: early XVI century) *Choir, Winchester Cathedral.*

Heraldic boss with the coat of arms of Henry VII.

BACK COVER

This XII-century sandstone corbel, now in the Victoria and Albert Museum, is an example of the grotesque stone-carving, the best examples of which still *in situ* can be seen, for instance, on Winchester Cathedral (south transept, *c.* 1107), at Romsey Abbey (*c.* 1120) and at Kilpeck, in Herefordshire (1140-50).

INDIVIDUAL ACKNOWLEDGMENTS

British Museum	Plates 3 and 37
B. Burwell	Plate 40
C. J. P. Cave	Front cover. Plates 1 and 56
F. H. Crossley	Plates 32, 38, 48, 49, 50
Arthur Gardner	Plates 28, 29, 39, 47
Mrs. R. Marcousé	Plate 25
National Building Record	Plates 31, 35, 43a, 43b
Philips City Studio, Wells, Somerset	Plates 26, 27a, 27b
Royal Commission on Historical Monuments	Plate 51
Walter Scott, Bradford	Plate 30
Victoria and Albert Museum	Plates 4, 5, 8, 9, 10, 11, 12, 13, 14, 15, 18, 19, 36, 42a, 42b, 44, 45, 46, 54, 55, Back cover
Warburg Institute	Plates 2, 16, 17, 21, 23, 24, 33, 34, 41
Dr. G. Zarnecki	Plates 6, 20, 22